HAL•LEONARD
HARMONICA PLAY-ALONG

JAZZ CLASSICS

VOL. 15

APR 1 4 2014

Harmonica by Steve Cohen

ISBN 978-1-4234-7602-3

Visit Hal Leonard Online at
www.halleonard.com

HAL•LEONARD®
CORPORATION
7777 W. BLUEMOUND RD. P.O. BOX 13819
MILWAUKEE, WISCONSIN 53213

VOL. 15

JAZZ CLASSICS

CONTENTS

HARMONICA NOTATION LEGEND

Harmonica music can be notated two different ways: on a *musical staff*, and in *tablature*.

THE MUSICAL STAFF shows pitches and rhythms and is divided by bar lines into measures. Pitches are named after the first seven letters of the alphabet.

TABLATURE graphically represents the harmonica music. Each note will be accompanied by a number, 1 through 10, indicating what hole you are to play. The arrow that follows indicates whether to blow or draw. (All examples are shown using a C diatonic harmonica.)

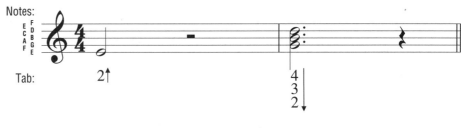

Blow (exhale) into 2nd hole.

Draw (inhale) 2nd, 3rd, & 4th holes together.

Notes on the C Harmonica

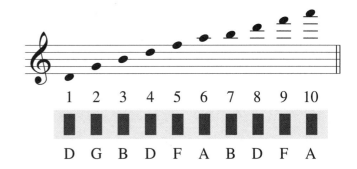

Exhaled (Blown) Notes

1 2 3 4 5 6 7 8 9 10

C E G C E G C E G C

Inhaled (Drawn) Notes

1 2 3 4 5 6 7 8 9 10

D G B D F A B D F A

Bends

Blow Bends

- 1/4 step
- 1/2 step
- 1 step
- 1 1/2 steps

Draw Bends

- 1/4 step
- 1/2 step
- 1 step
- 1 1/2 steps

Definitions for Special Harmonica Notation

SLURRED BEND: Play (draw) 3rd hole, then bend the note down one whole step.

GRACE NOTE BEND: Starting with a pre-bent note, immediately release bend to the target note.

VIBRATO: Begin adding vibrato to the sustained note on beat 3.

TONGUE BLOCKING: Using your tongue to block holes 2 & 3, play octaves on holes 1 & 4.

TRILL: Shake the harmonica rapidly to alternate between notes.

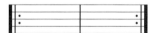

NOTE: Tablature numbers in parentheses are used when:

- The note is sustained, but a new articulation begins (such as vibrato), or
- The quantity of notes being sustained changes, or
- A change in dynamics (volume) occurs.
- It's the alternate note in a trill.

Additional Musical Definitions

D.S. al Coda
- Go back to the sign (%), then play until the measure marked "***To Coda***," then skip to the section labelled "**Coda**."

D.C. al Fine
- Go back to the beginning of the song and play until the measure marked "***Fine***" (end).

- Repeat measures between signs.

 *(accent)*
- Accentuate the note (play initial attack louder).

(staccato)
- Play the note short.

- When a repeated section has different endings, play the first ending only the first time and the second ending only the second time.

Dynamics

p
- Piano (soft)

mp
- Mezzo Piano (medium soft)

mf
- Mezzo Forte (medium loud)

f
- Forte (loud)

(crescendo)
- Gradually louder

(decrescendo)
- Gradually softer

All Blues

By Miles Davis

A Intro

Moderately fast ♩ = 135

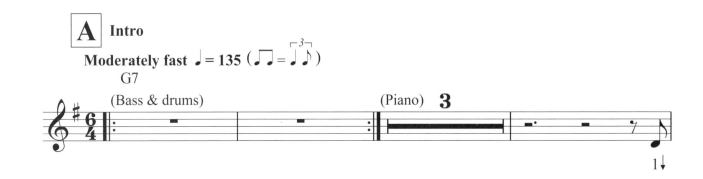

B Head

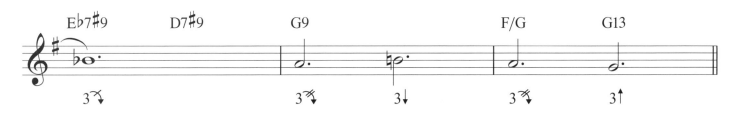

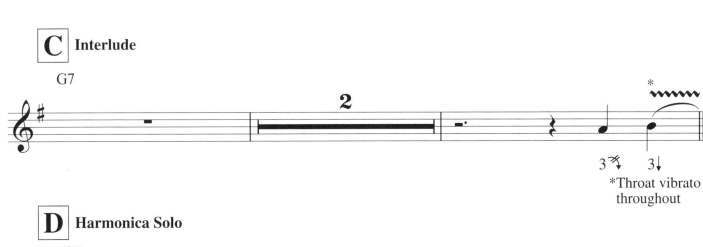

C Interlude

*Throat vibrato
throughout

D Harmonica Solo

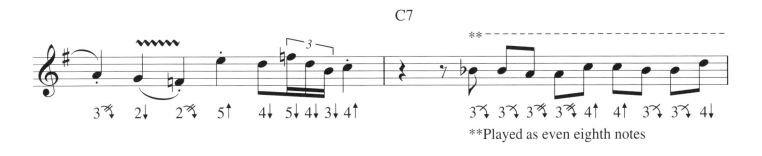

**Played as even eighth notes

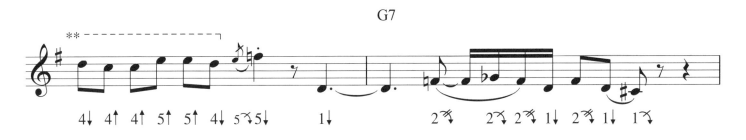

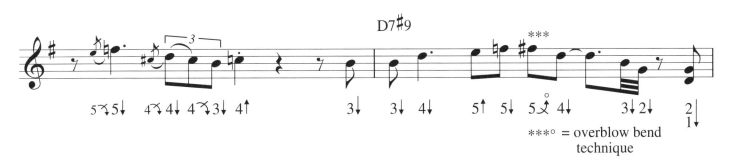

***° = overblow bend
technique

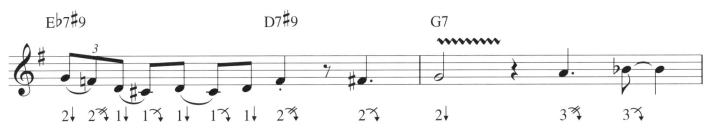

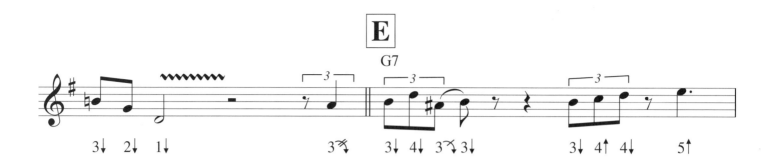

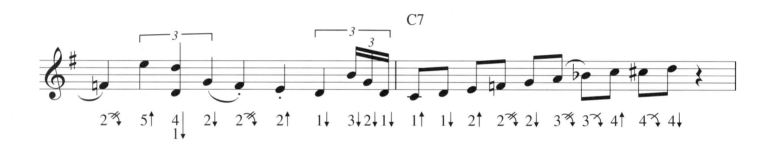

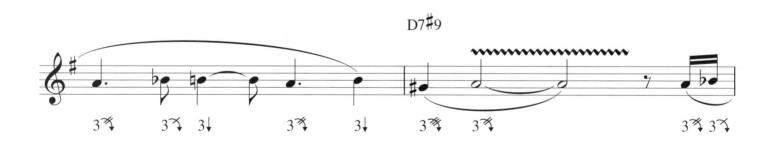

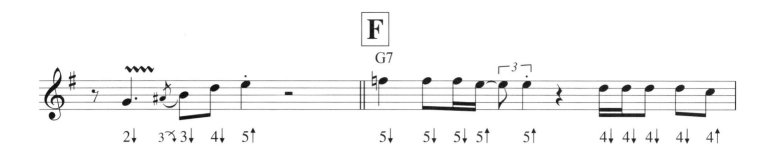

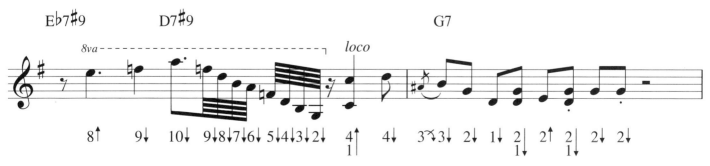

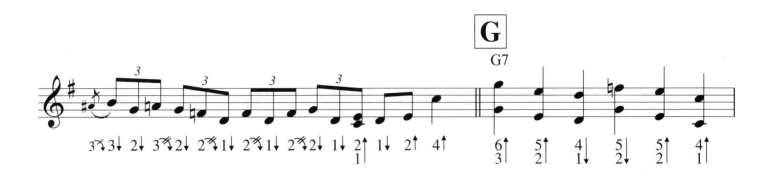

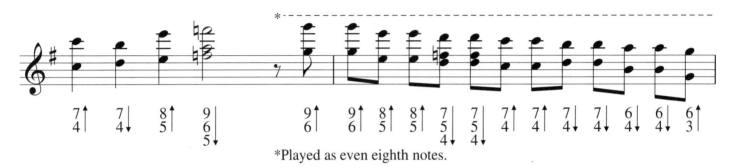

*Played as even eighth notes.

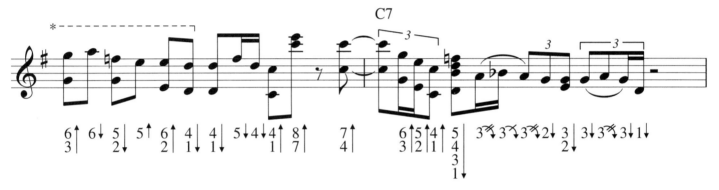

**Played as even eighths.

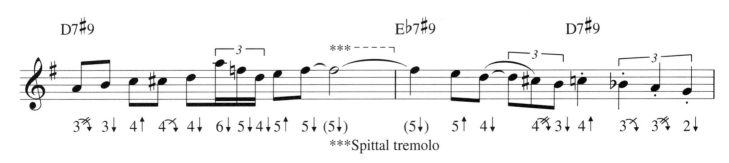

***Spittal tremolo

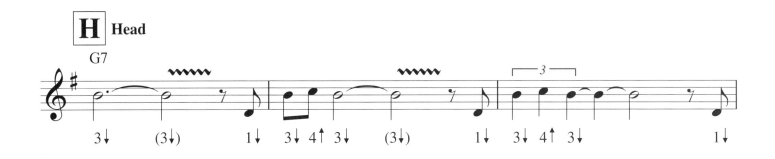

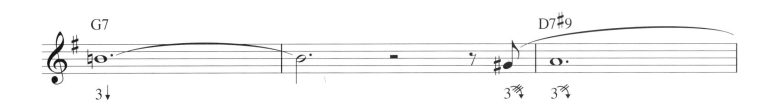

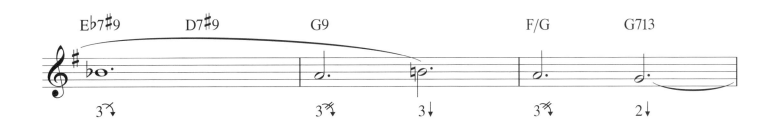

Au Privave

By Charlie Parker

A Head

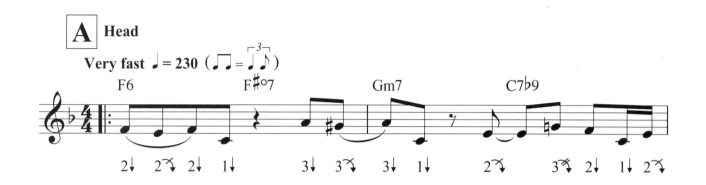

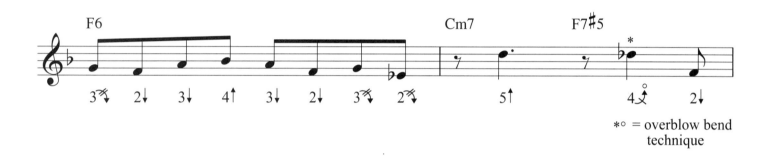

*° = overblow bend technique

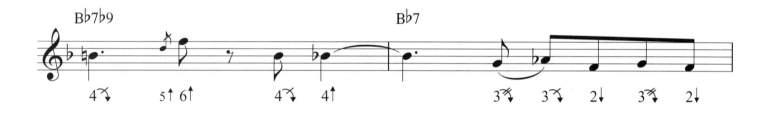

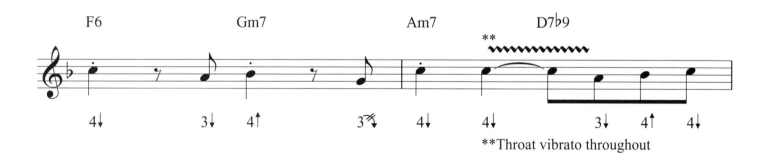

**Throat vibrato throughout

B Harmonica Solo

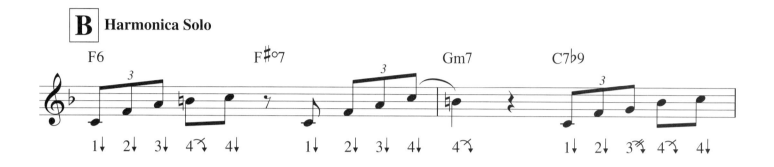

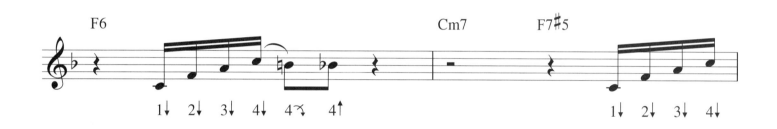

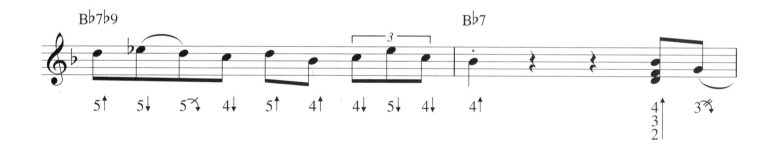

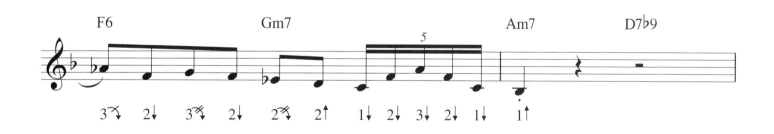

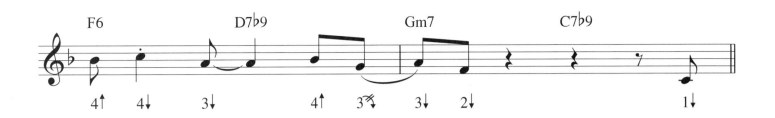

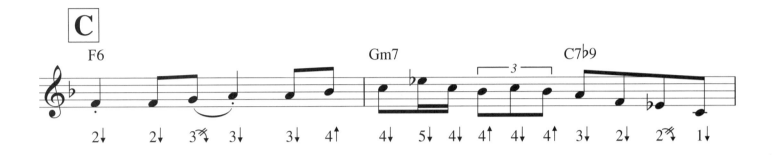

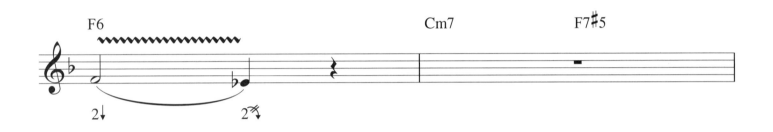

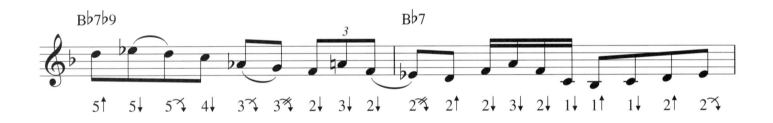

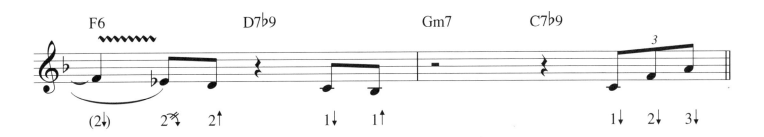

D

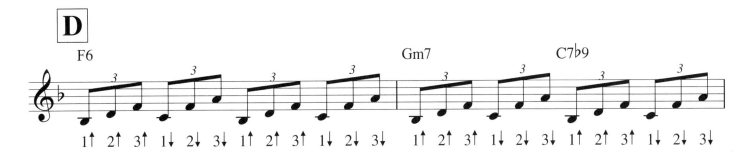

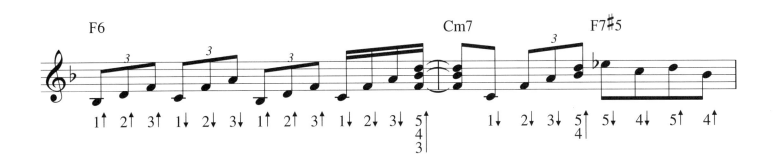

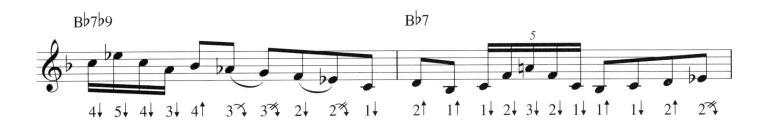

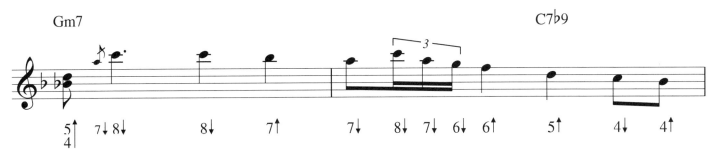

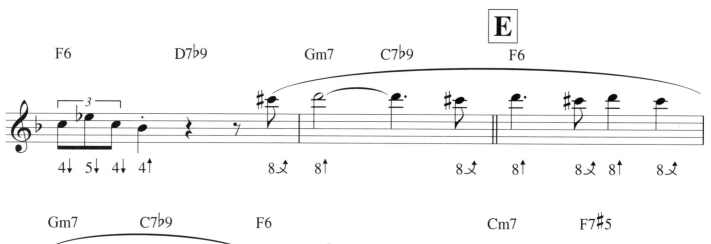

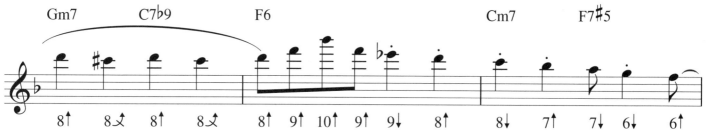

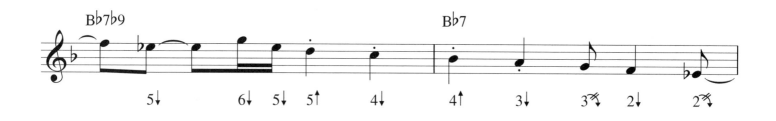

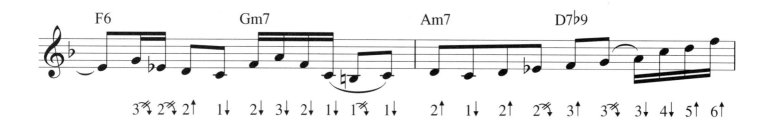

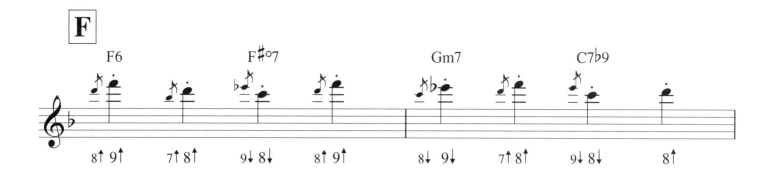

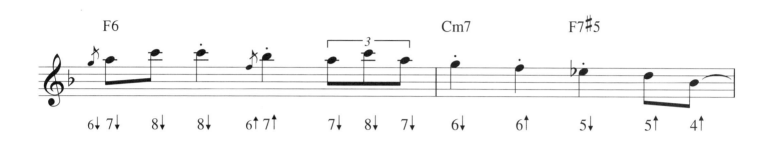

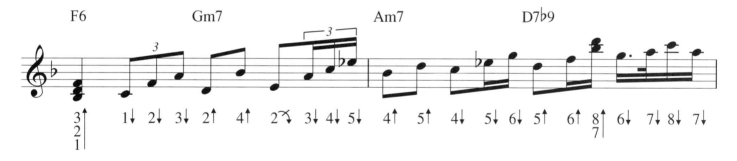

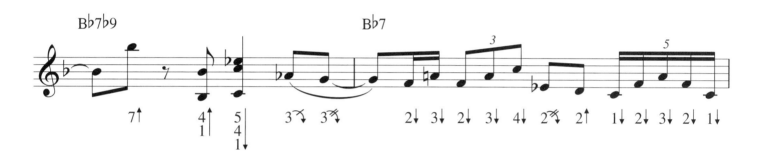

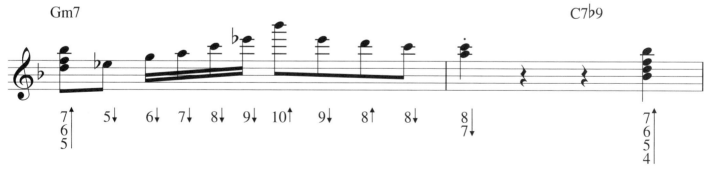

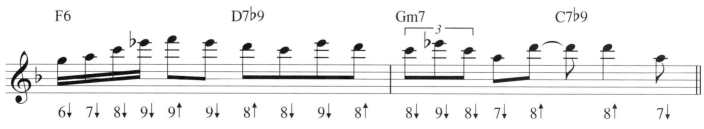

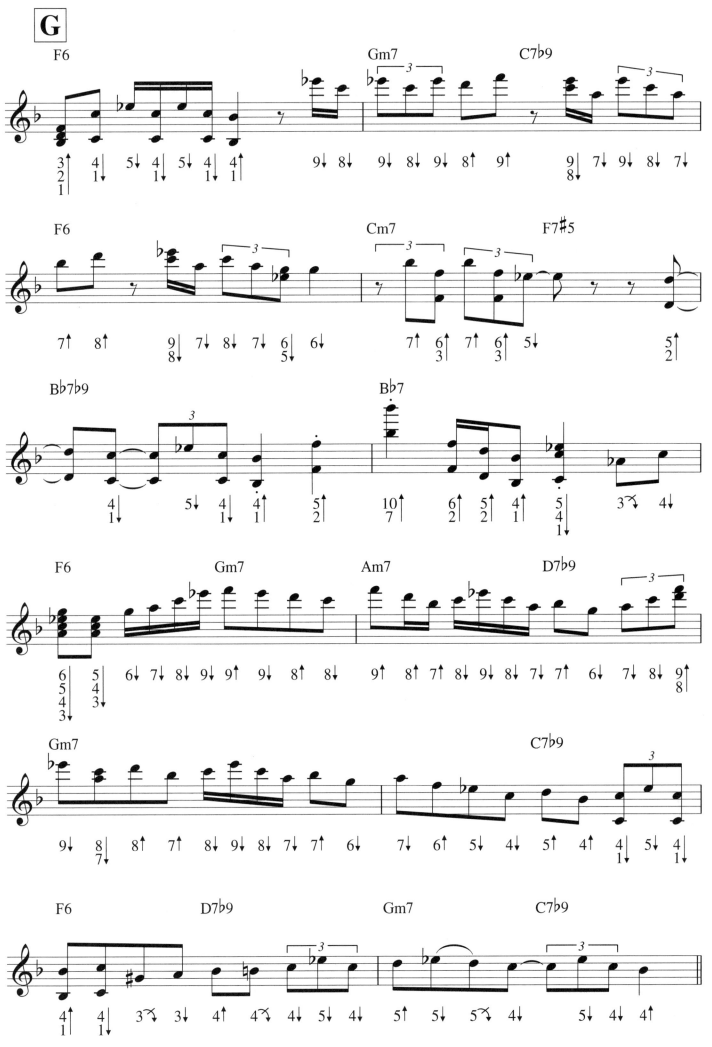

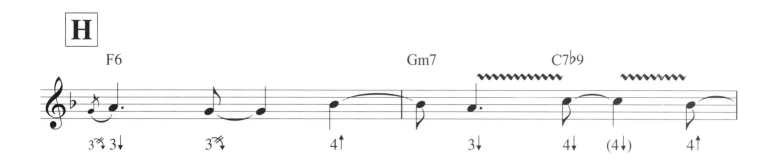

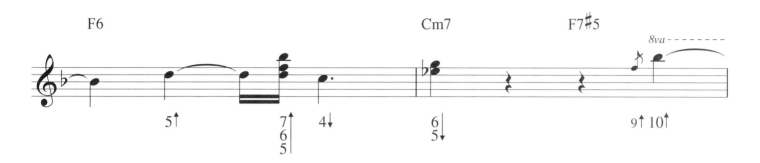

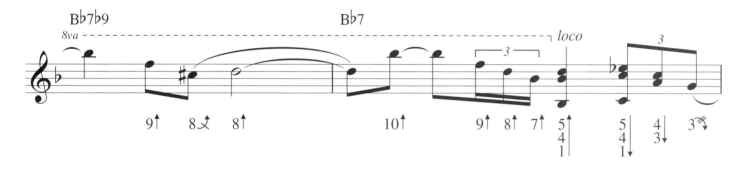

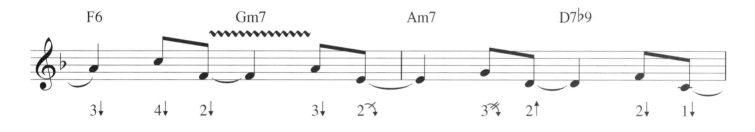

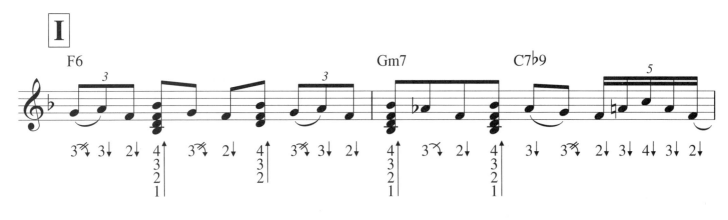

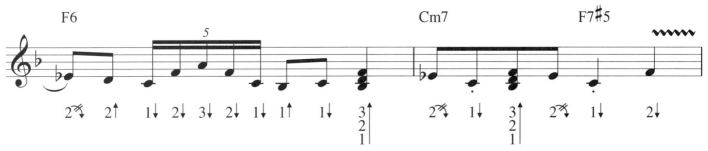

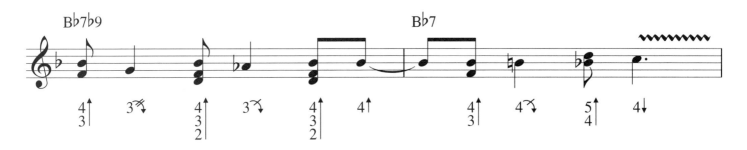

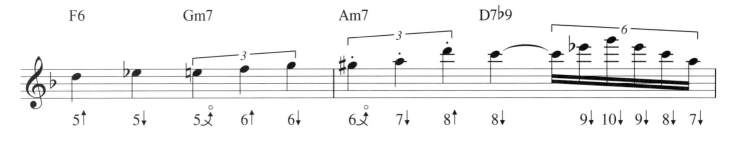

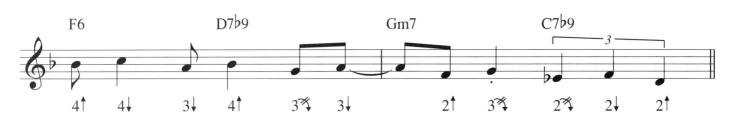

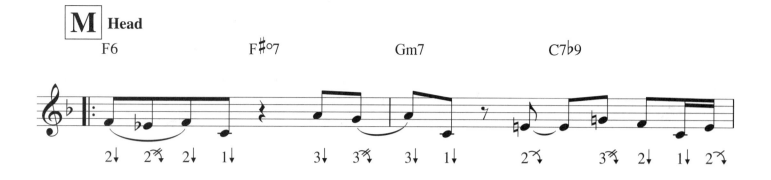

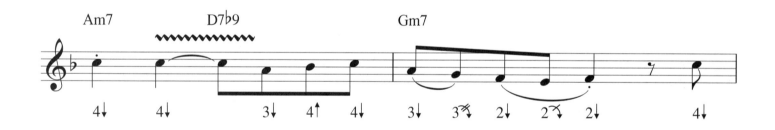

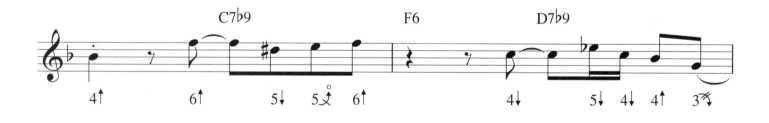

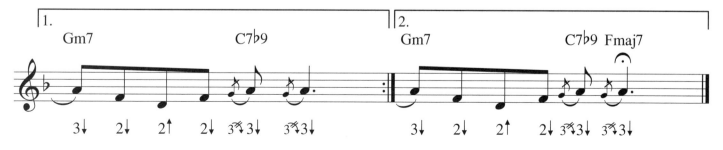

Song for My Father

Words and Music by Horace Silver

HARMONICA

Harp Keys: A♭ and B♭ Diatonic

A Intro

Moderately ♩ = 124

Fm7

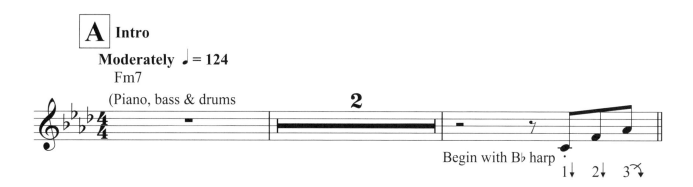

(Piano, bass & drums

Begin with B♭ harp

B Head

Fm7

*Throat vibrato

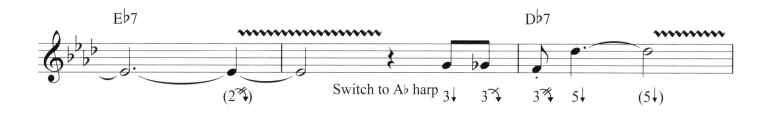

E♭7   D♭7

Switch to A♭ harp

1.   2.

C7 N.C.   Fm11

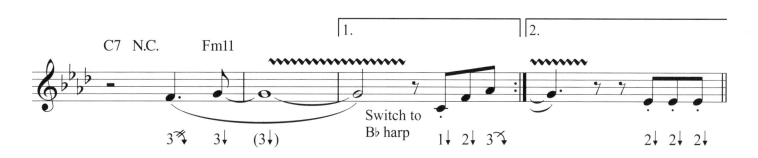

Switch to B♭ harp

Switch to B♭ harp

C

E♭7   Fm7

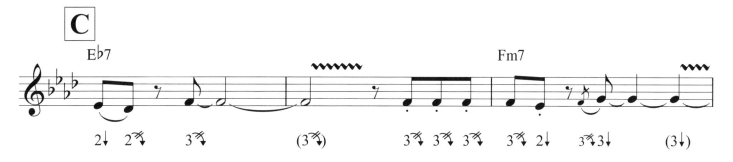

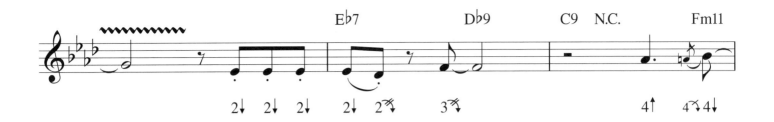

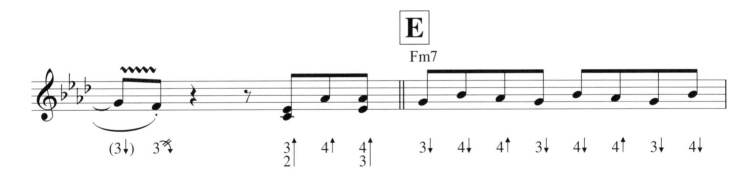

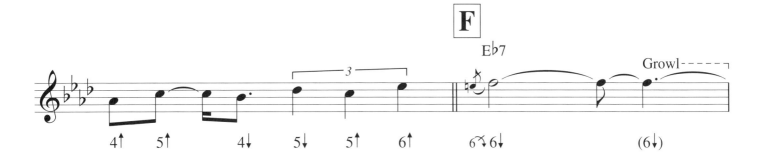

F

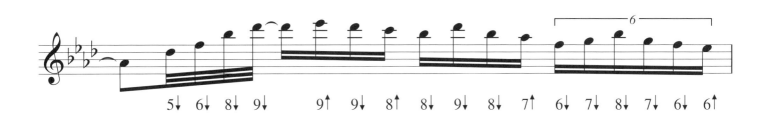

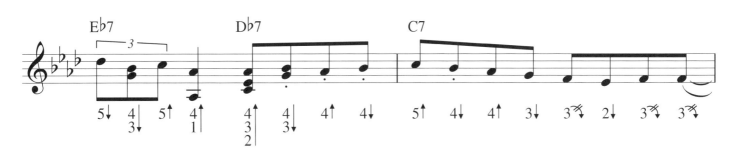

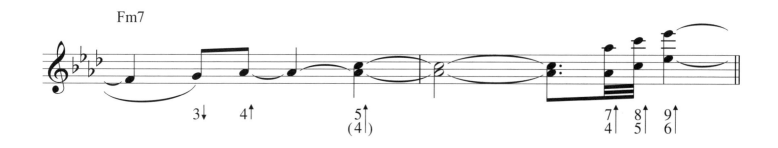

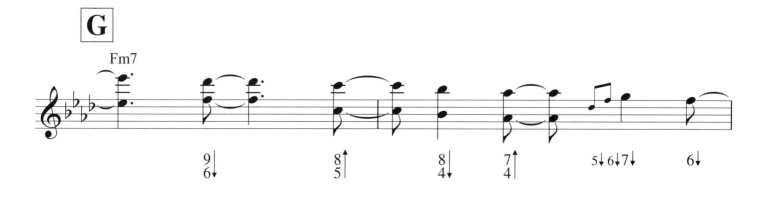

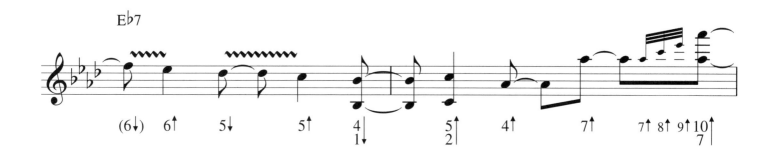

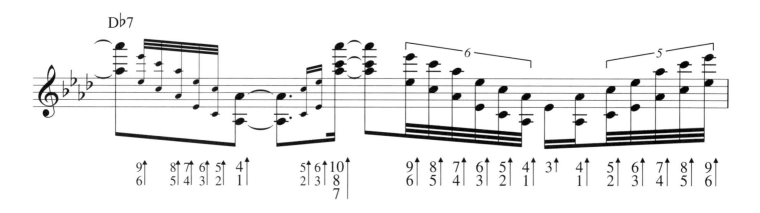

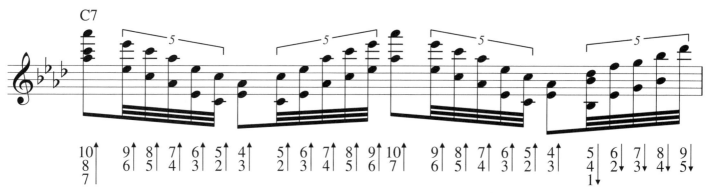

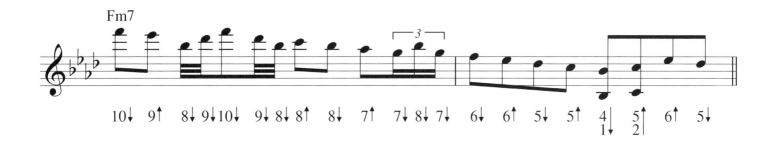

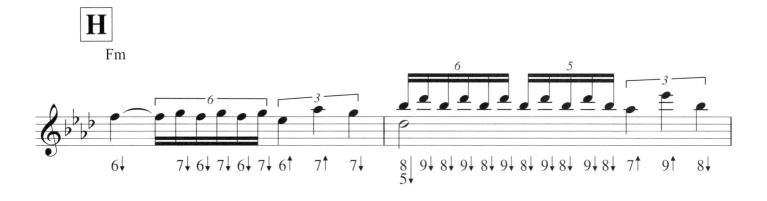

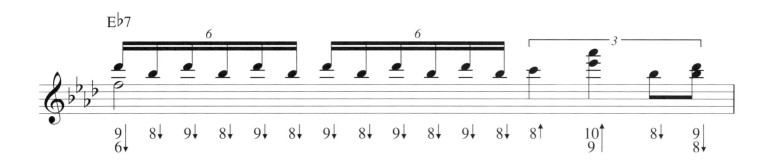

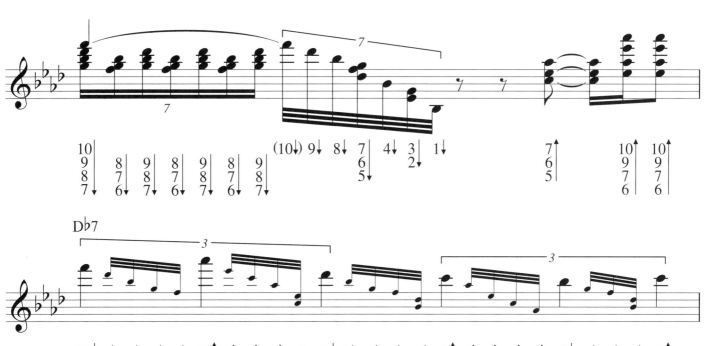

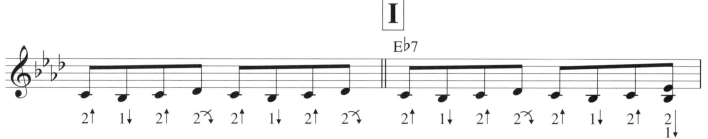

I

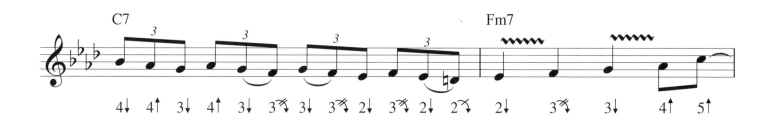

J Head

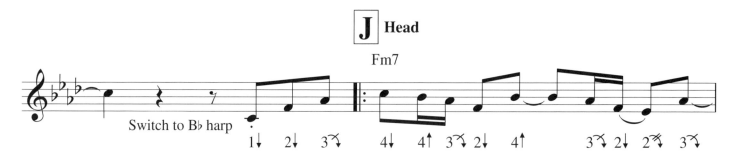

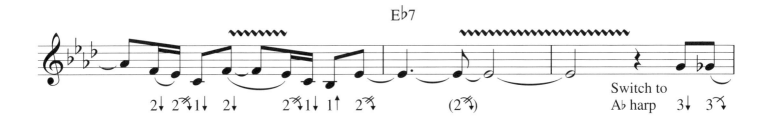

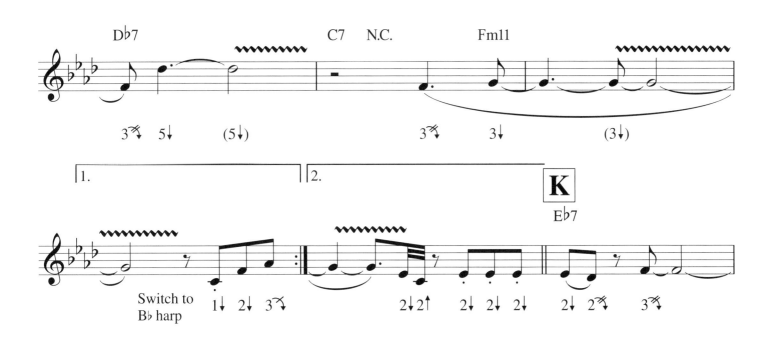

Comin' Home Baby

Words and Music by Robert Dorough and Benjamin Tucker

HARMONICA
Harp Key: C Diatonic

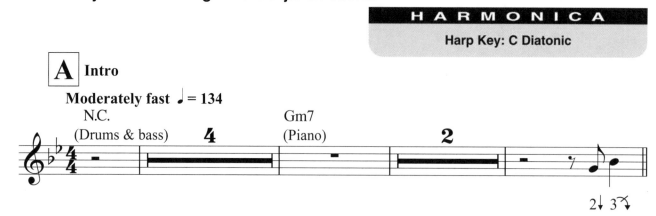

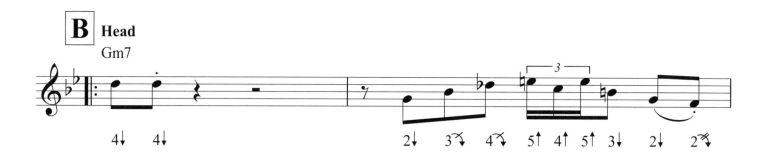

*Throat vibrato

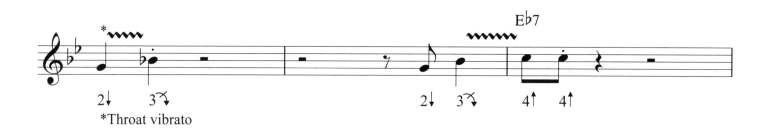

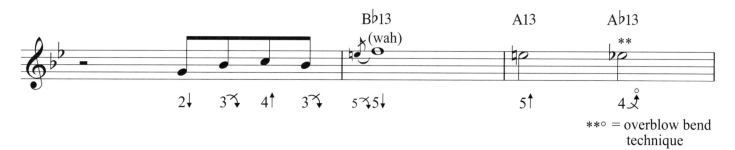

**° = overblow bend technique

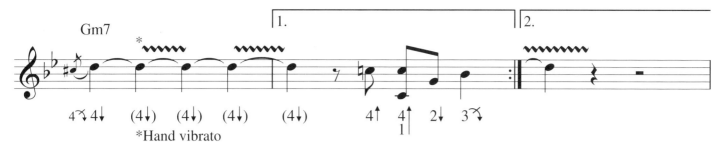

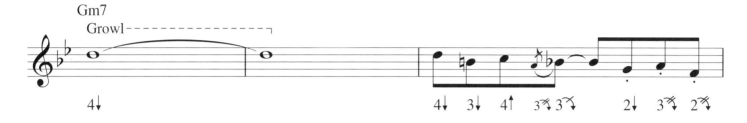

C **Harmonica Solo**

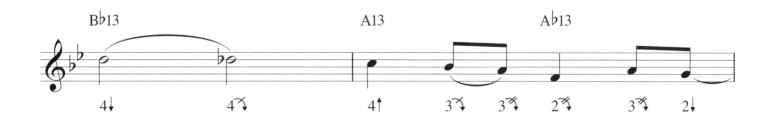

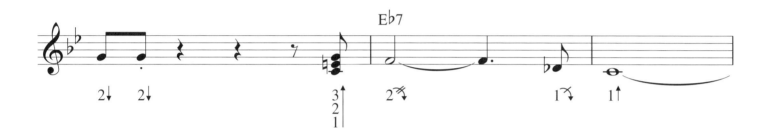

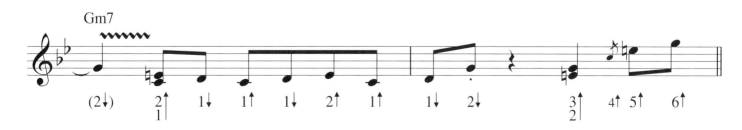

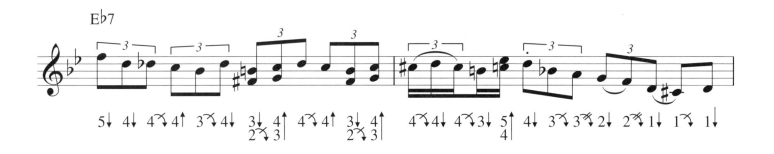

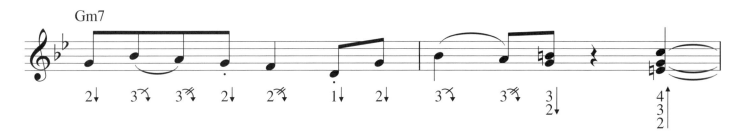

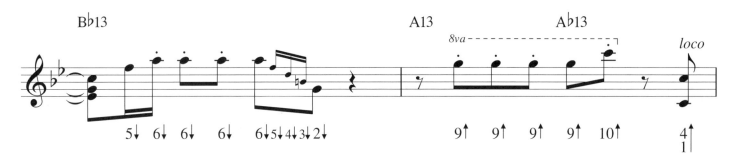

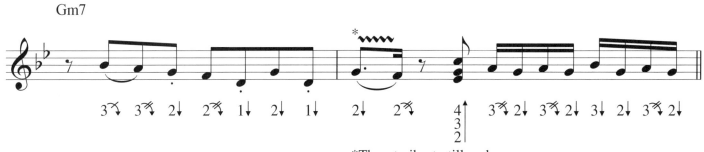

*Throat vibrato till end

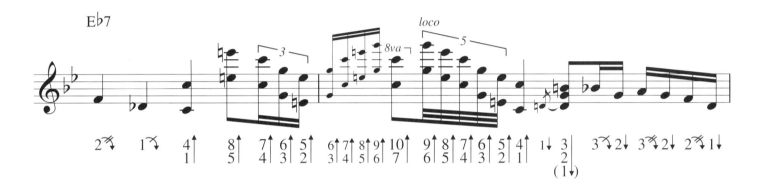

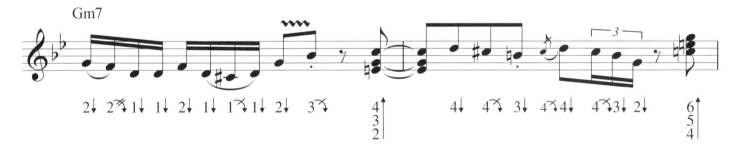

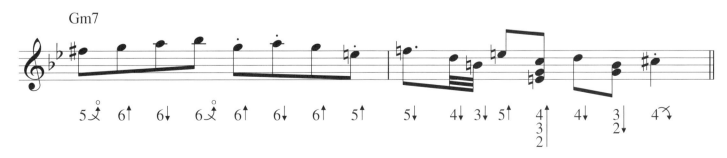

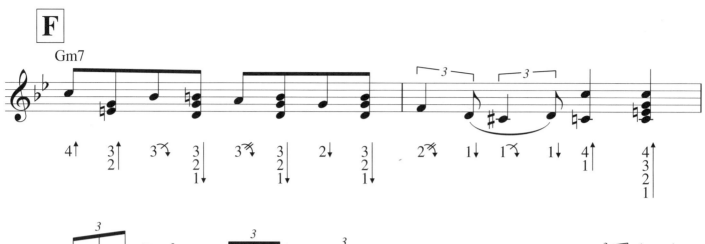

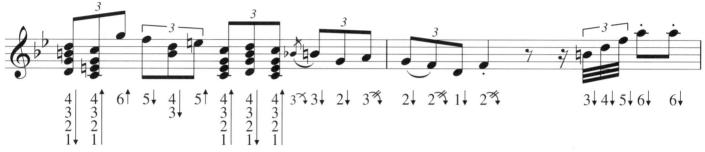

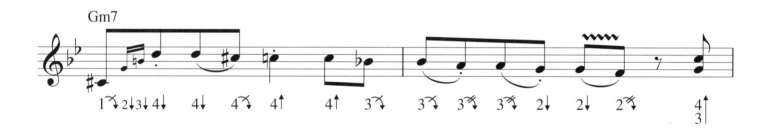

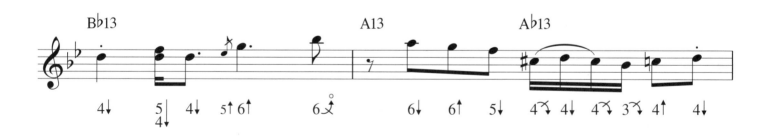

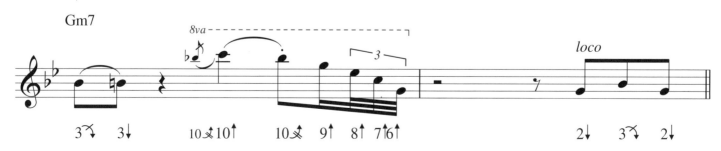

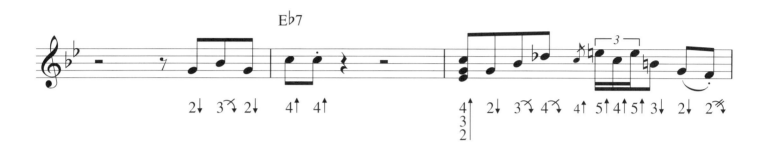

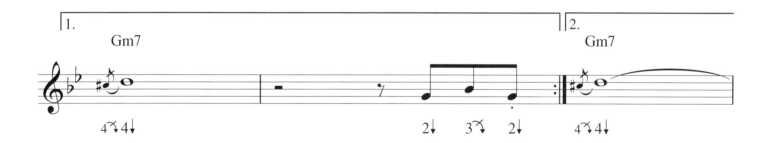

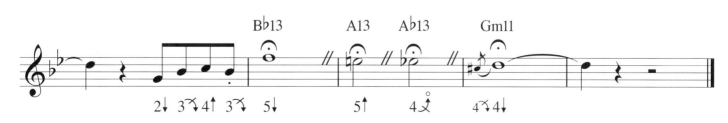

Sugar

By Stanley Turrentine

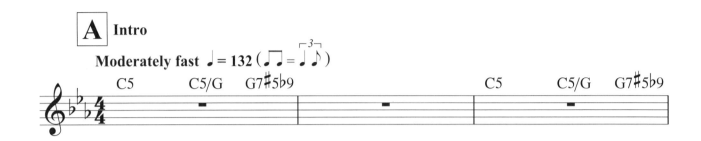

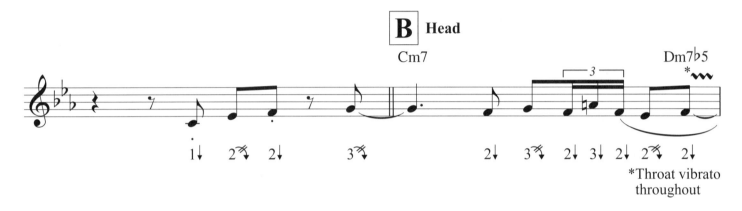

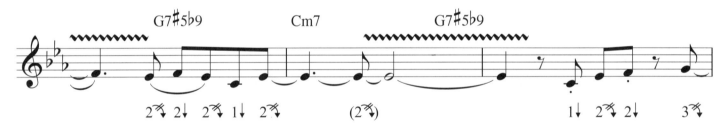

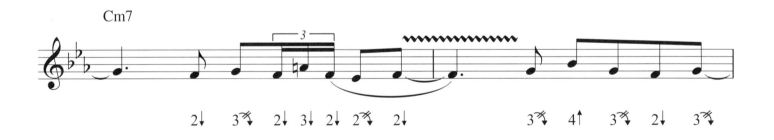

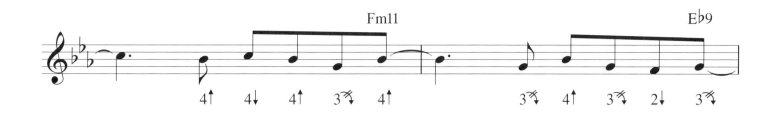

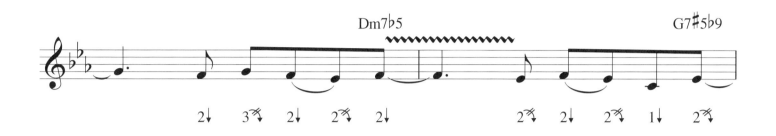

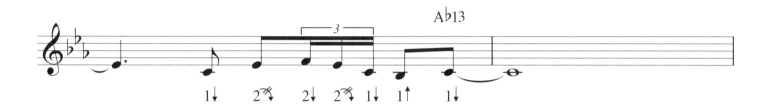

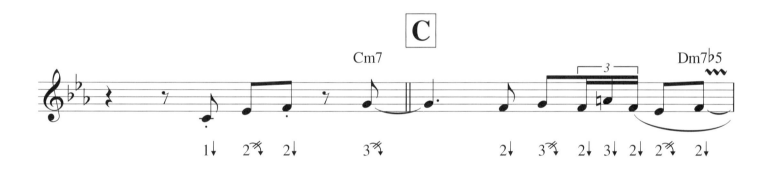

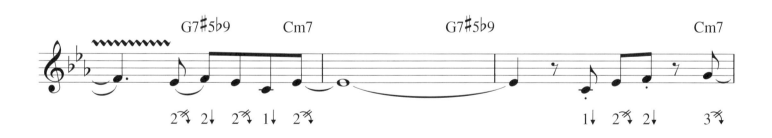

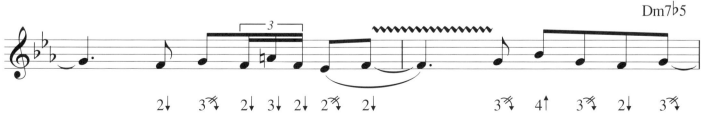

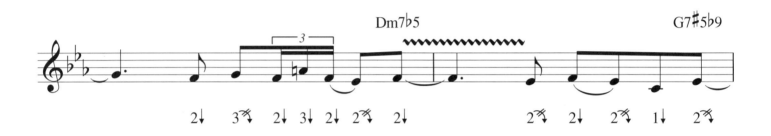

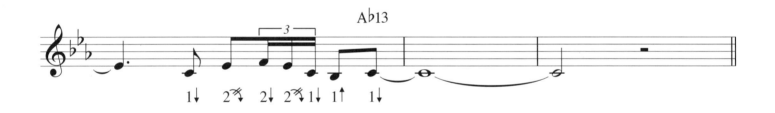

D **Harmonica Solo**

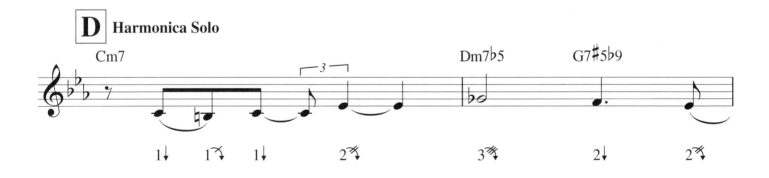

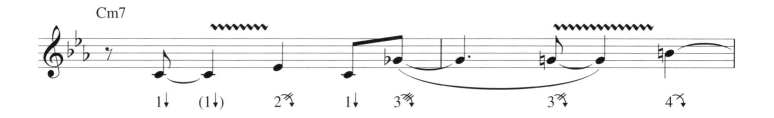

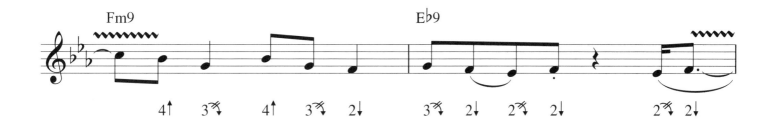

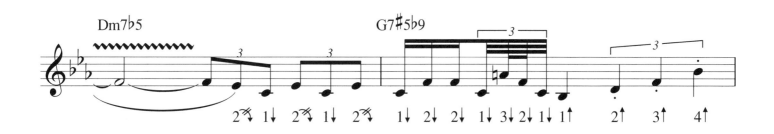

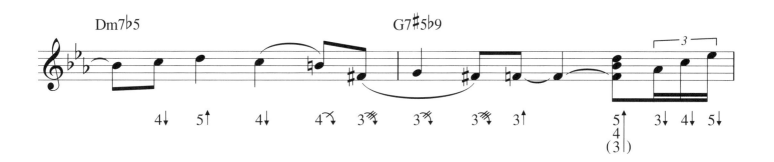

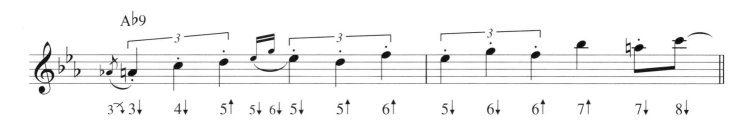

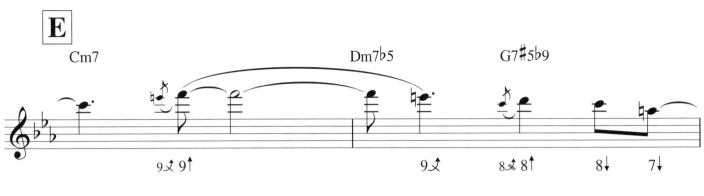

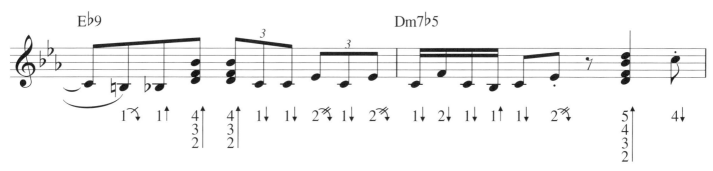

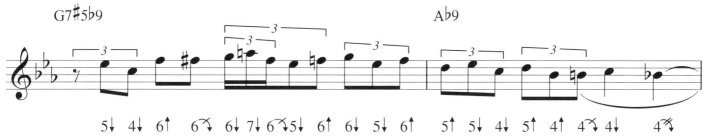

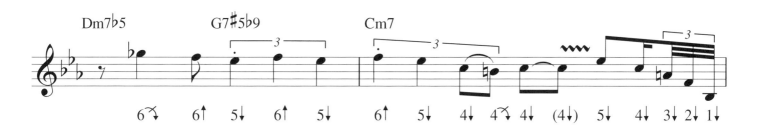

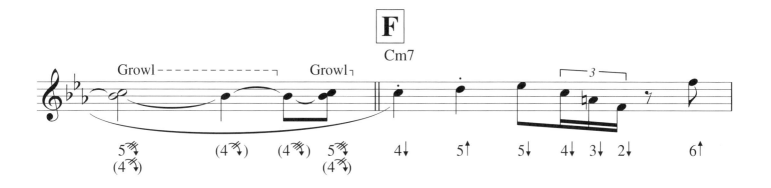

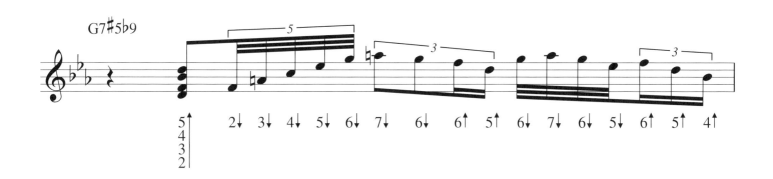

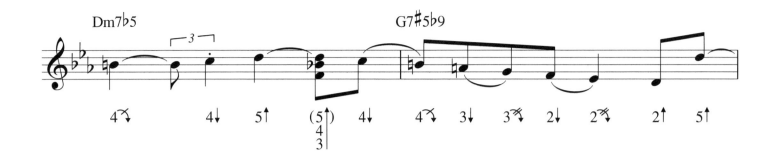

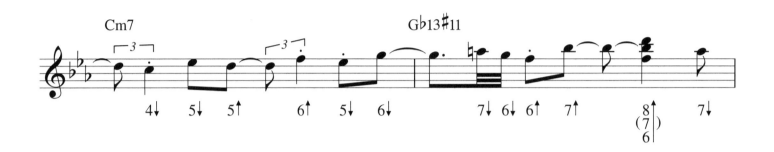

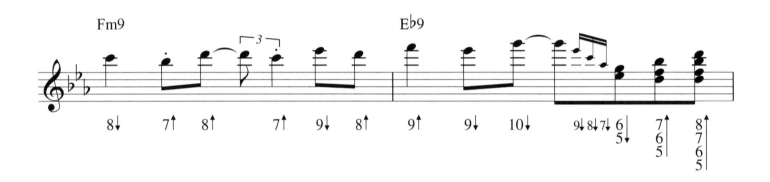

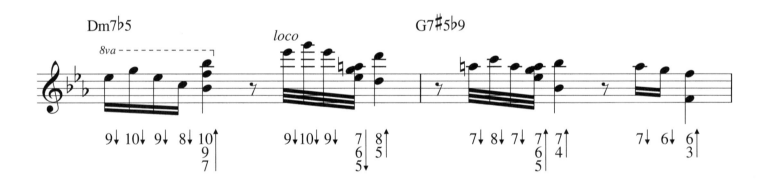

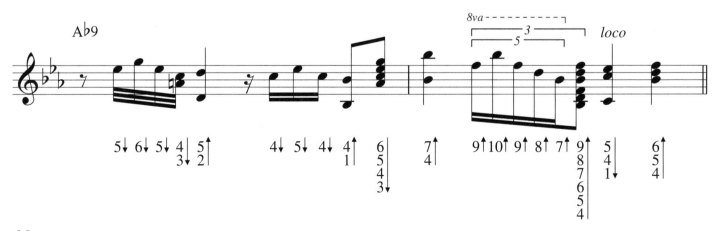

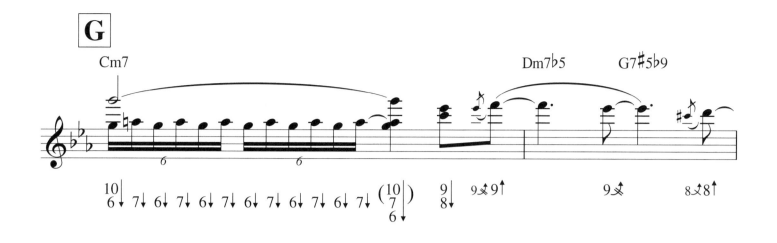

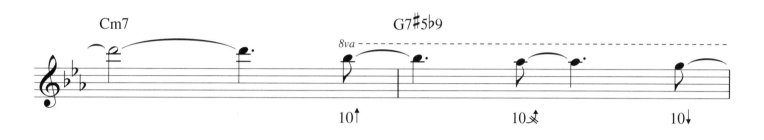

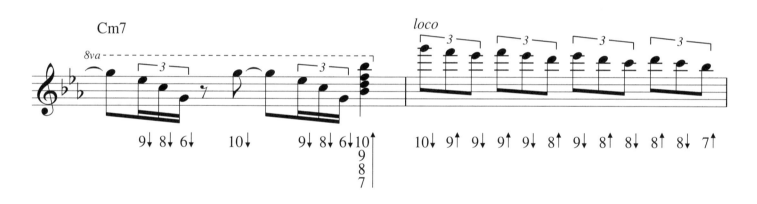

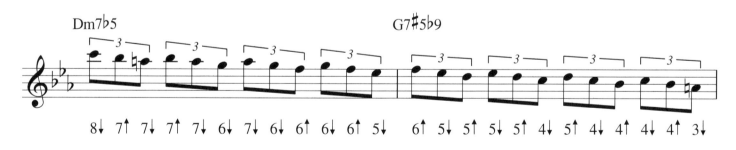

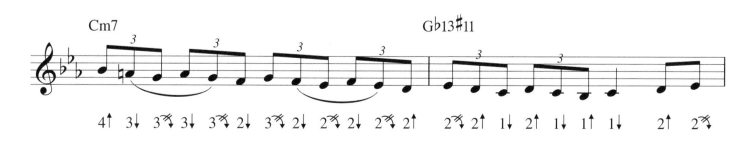

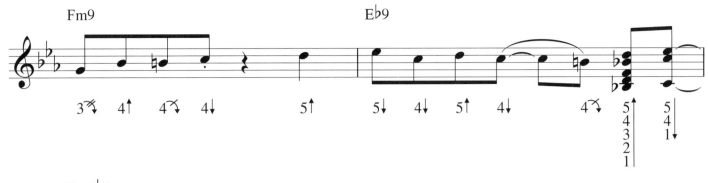

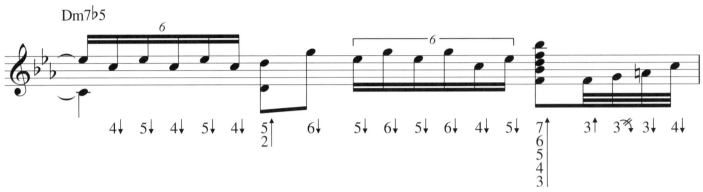

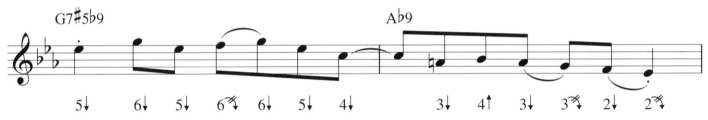

H Head

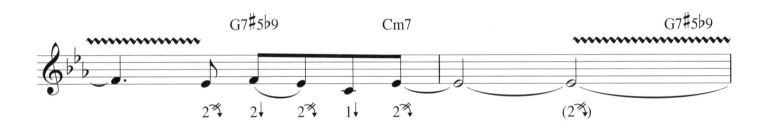

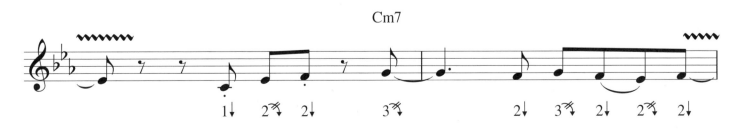

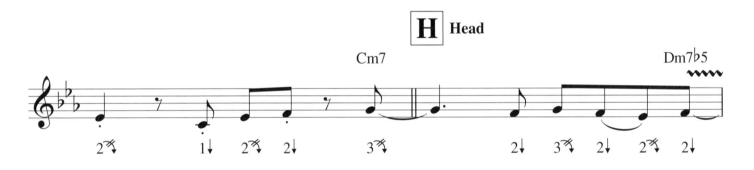

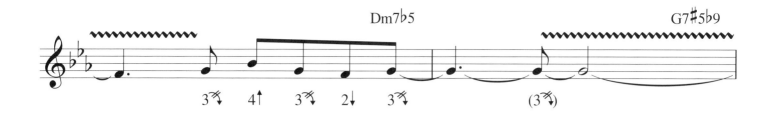

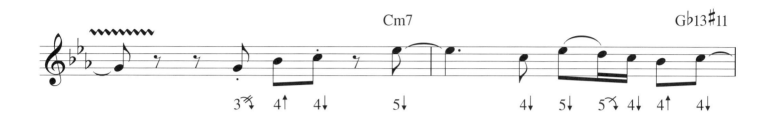

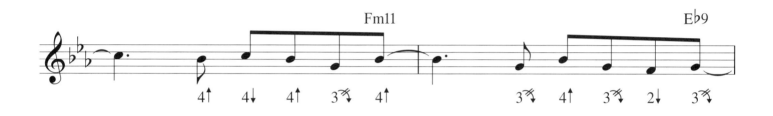

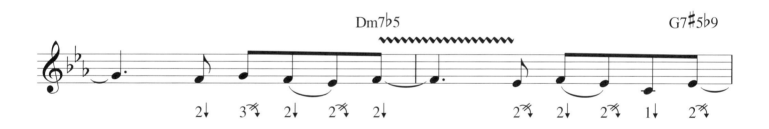

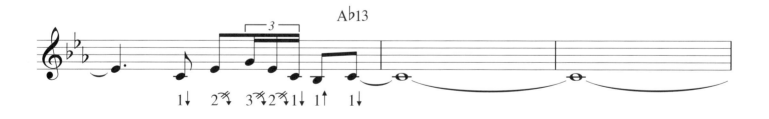

Free time

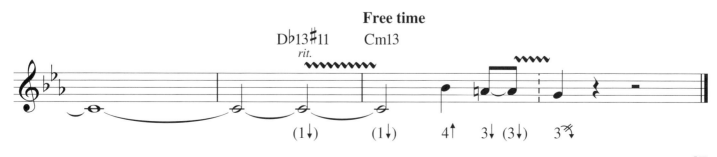

Sunny

Words and Music by Bobby Hebb

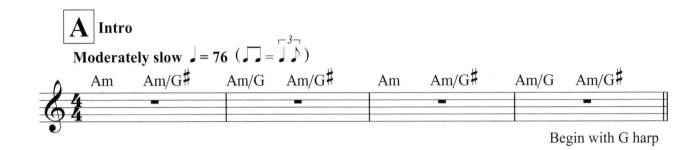

Begin with G harp

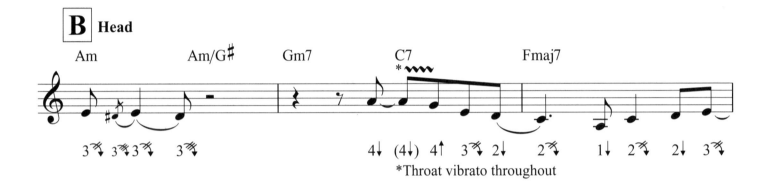

*Throat vibrato throughout

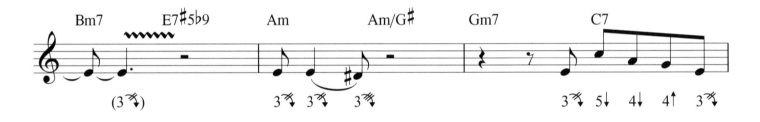

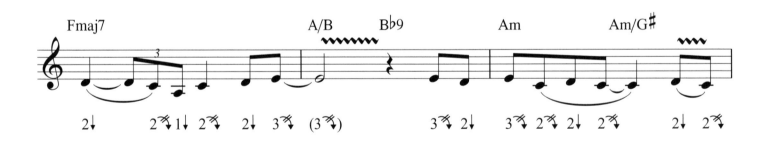

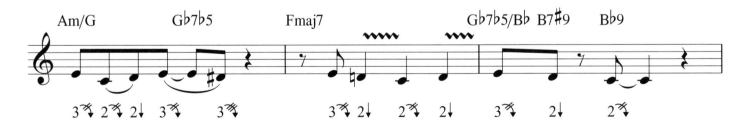

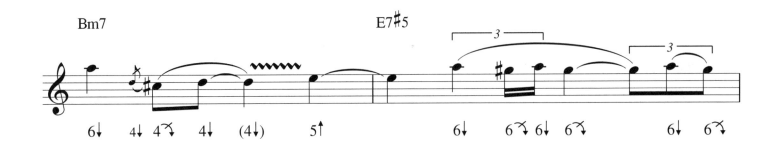

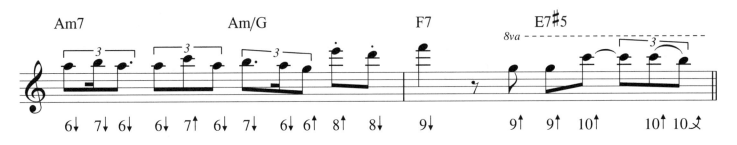

D

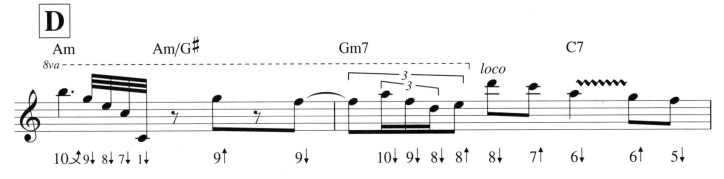

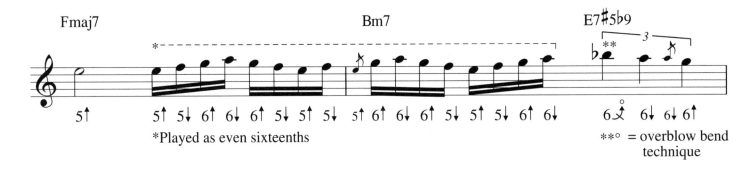

*Played as even sixteenths

**°* = overblow bend
technique

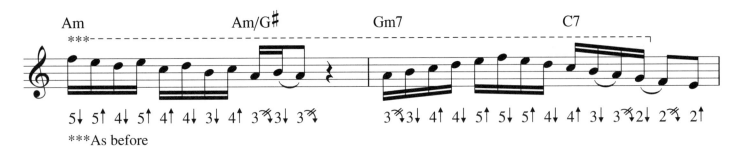

***As before

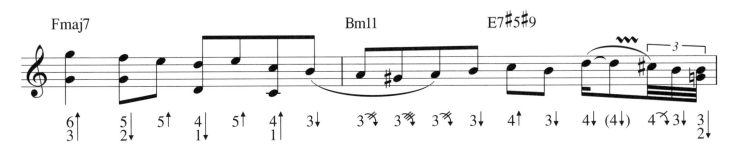

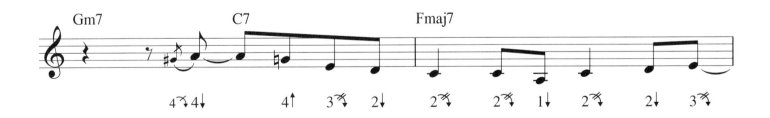

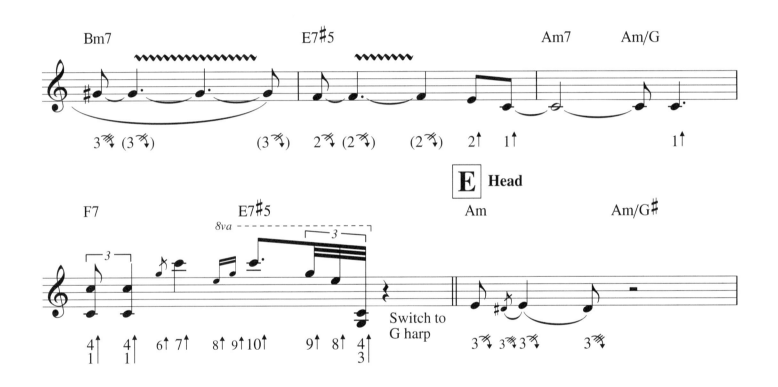

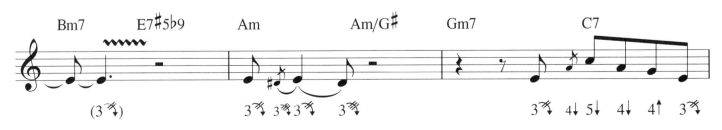

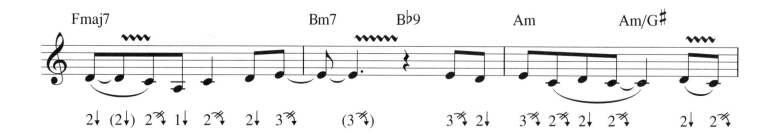

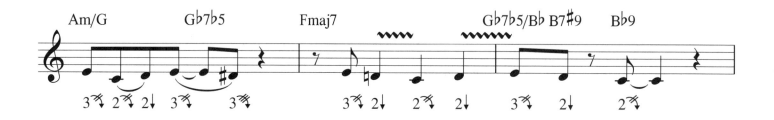

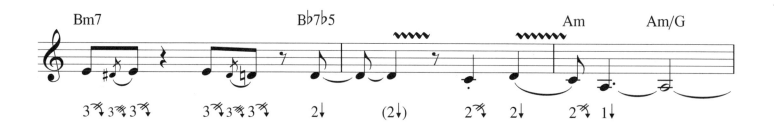

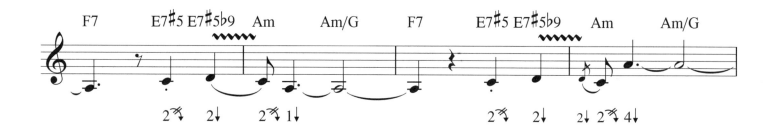

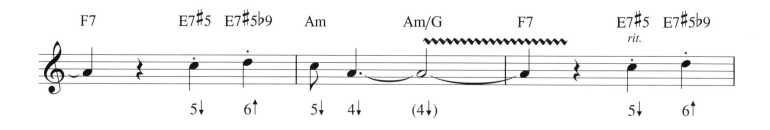

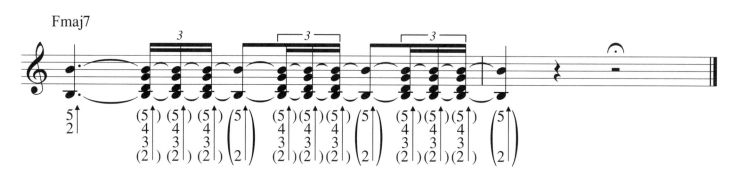

Take Five

By Paul Desmond

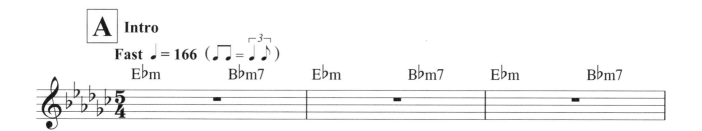

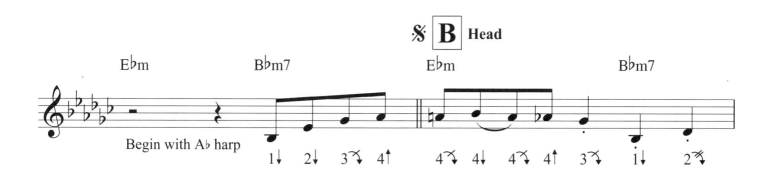

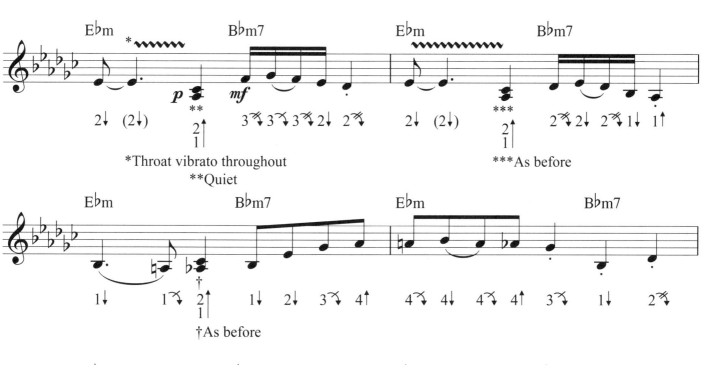

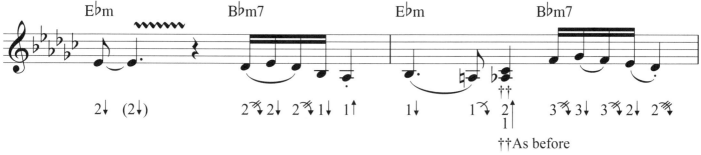

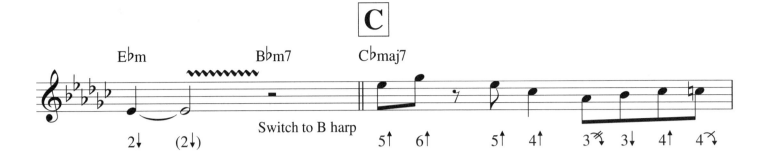

*° = overblow bend technique

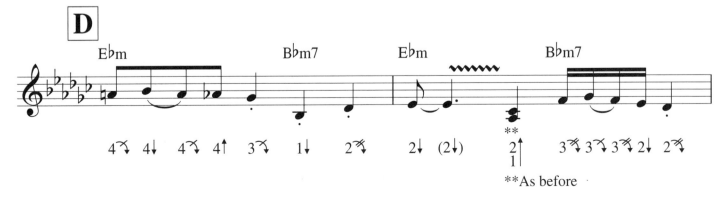

**As before

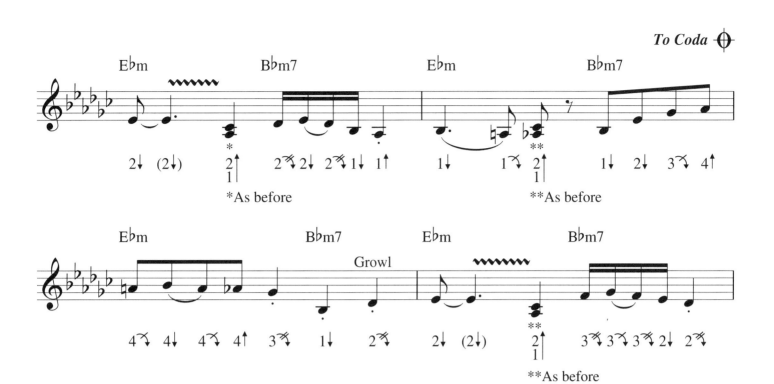

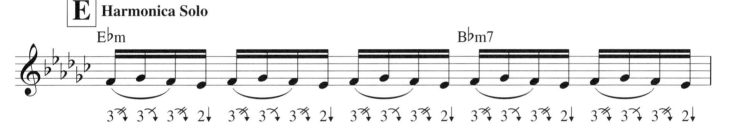

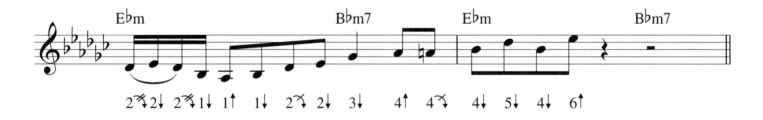

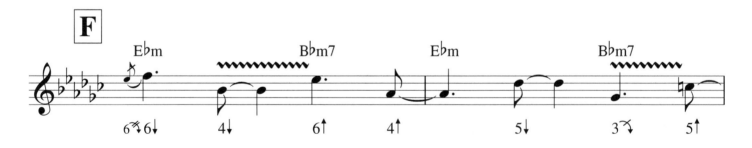

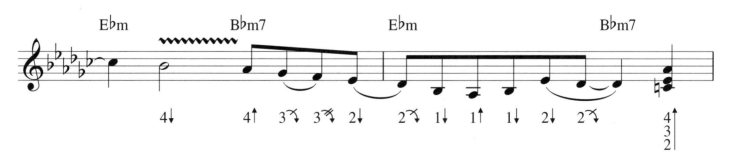

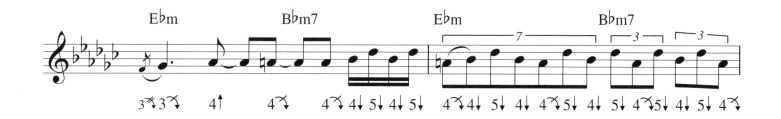

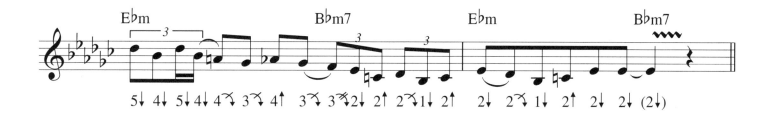

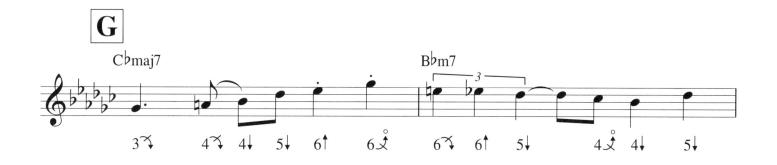

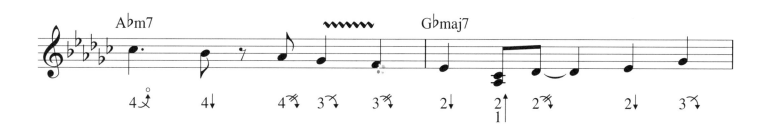

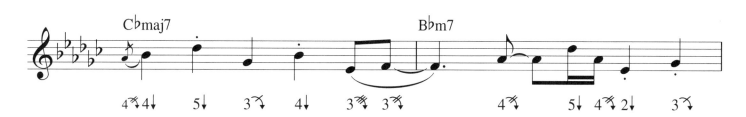

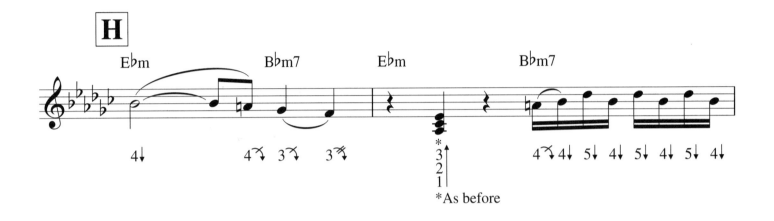

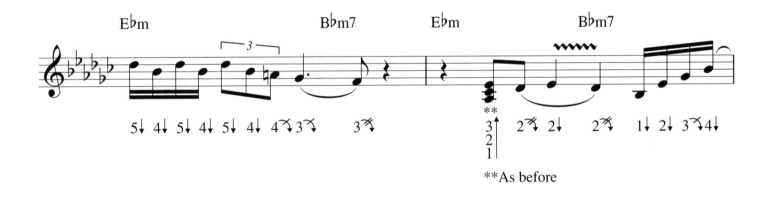

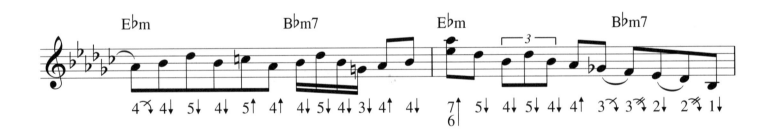

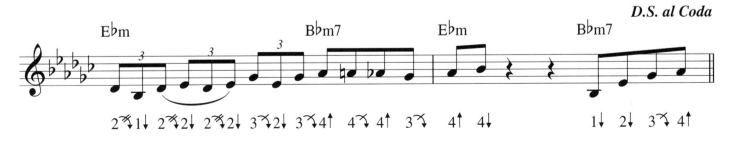

Work Song

Music by Nat Adderley

HARMONICA
Harp Key: B♭ Diatonic

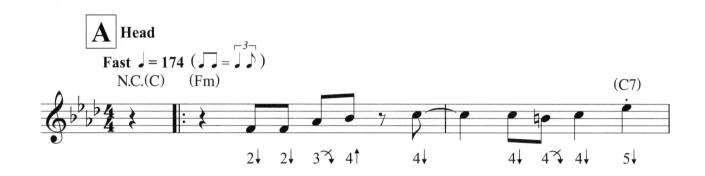

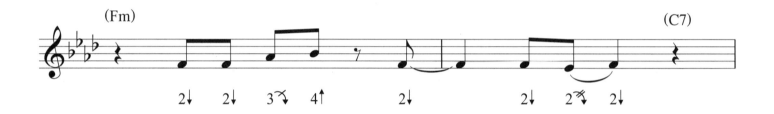

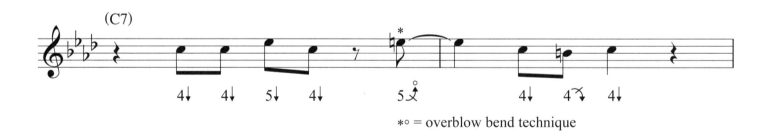

*○ = overblow bend technique

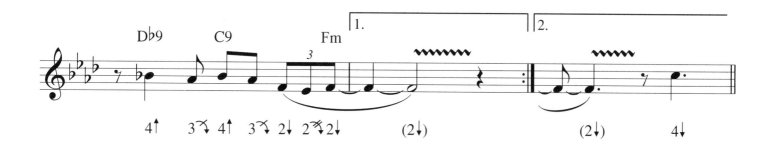

B Harmonica Solo

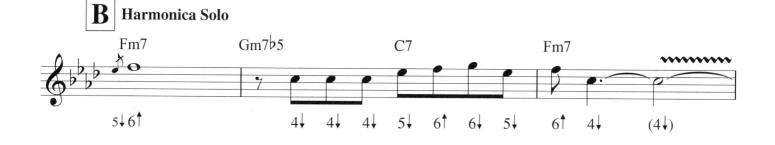

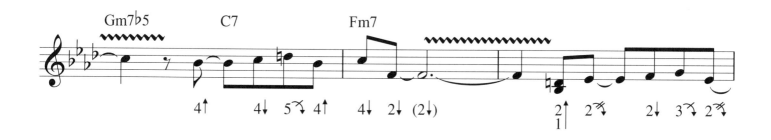

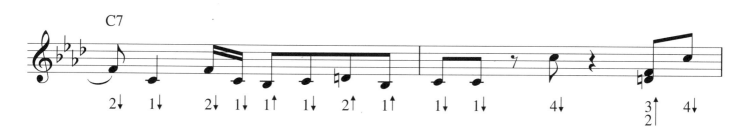

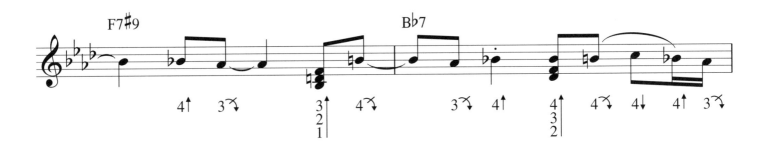

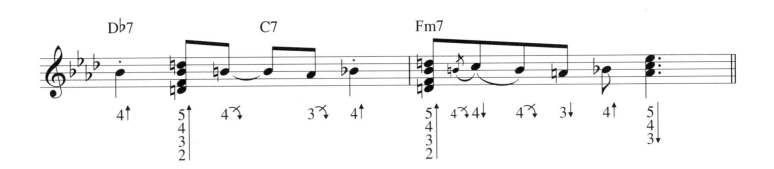

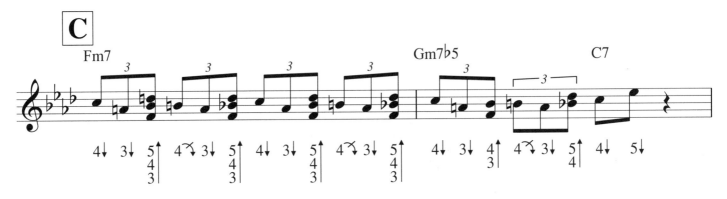

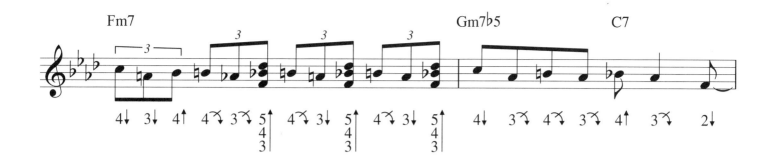

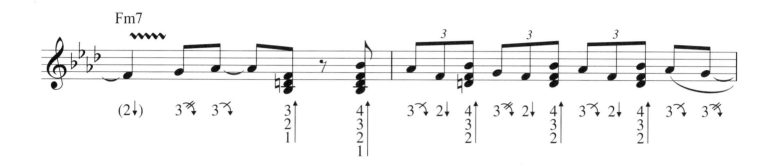

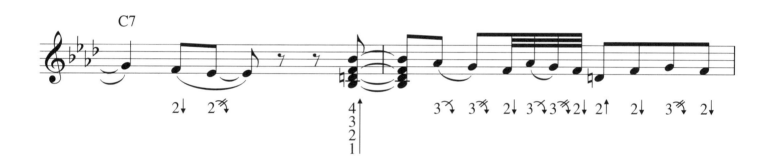

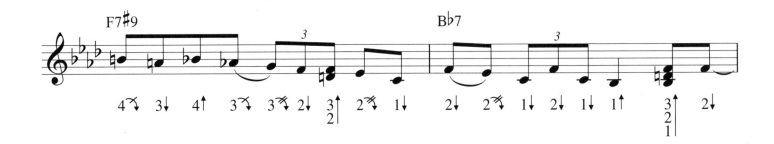

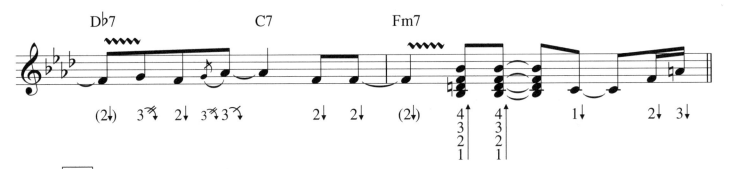

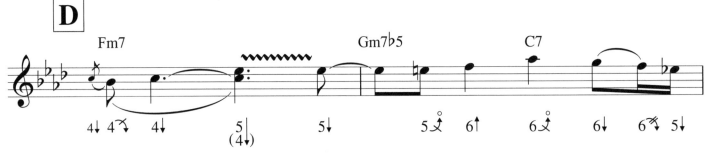

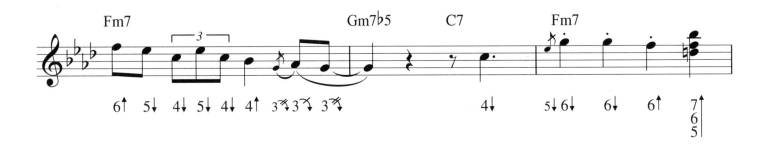

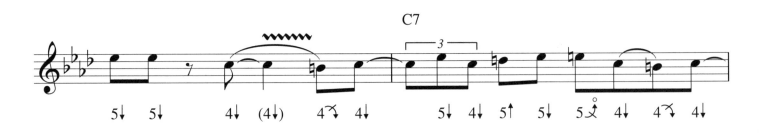

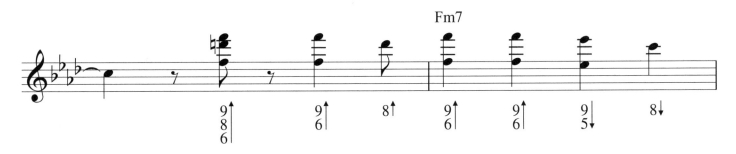

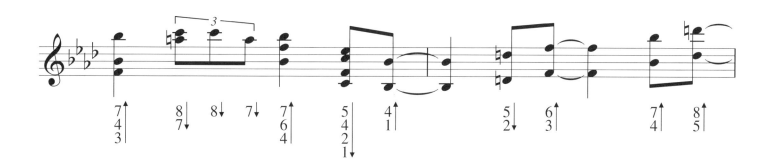

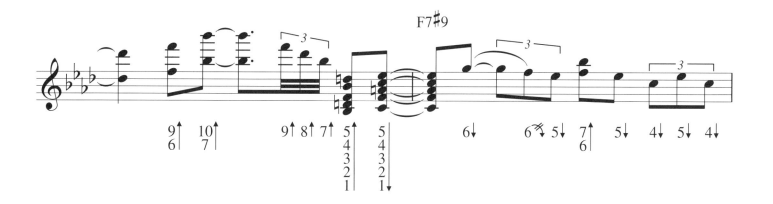

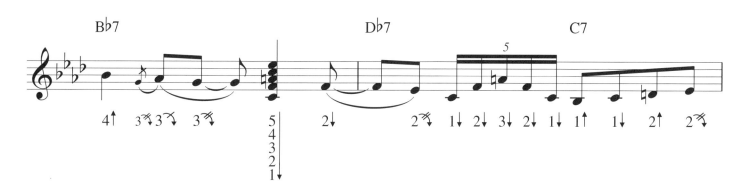

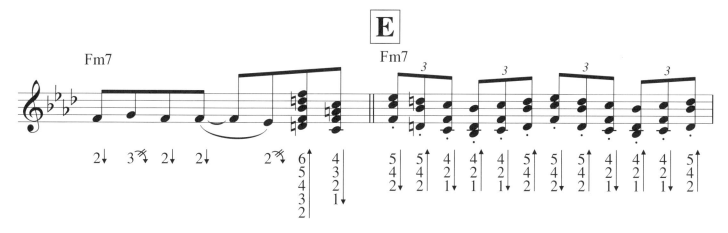

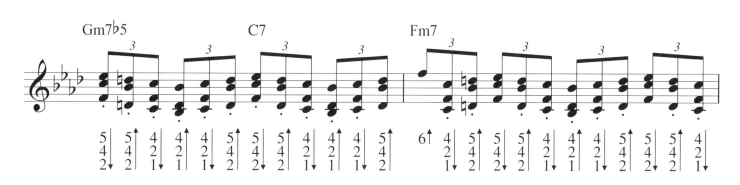

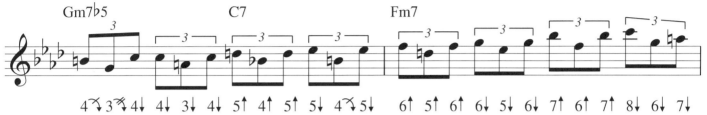

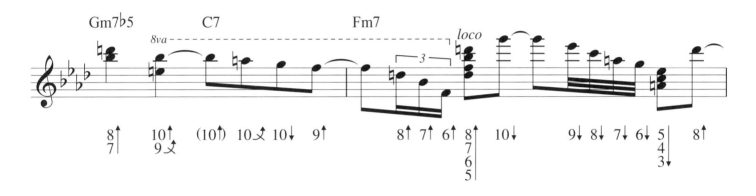

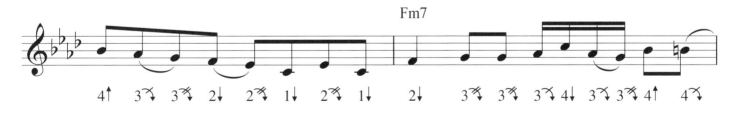

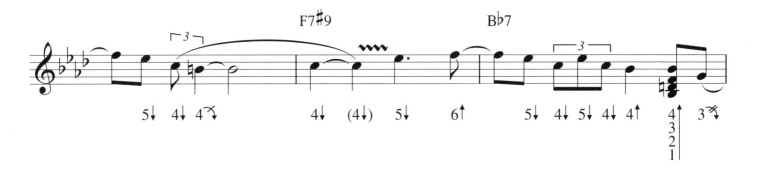

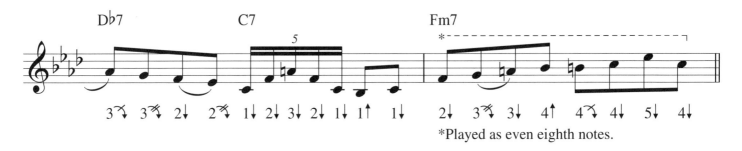

*Played as even eighth notes.

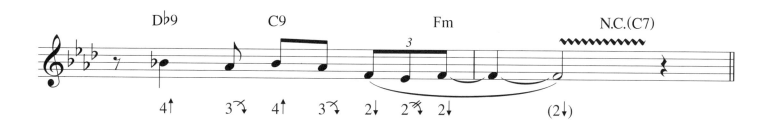

H

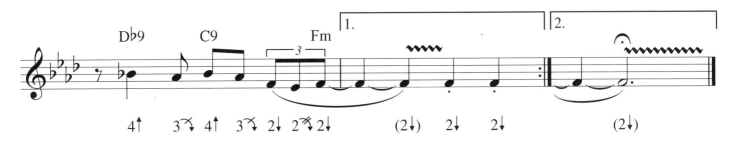

The Harmonica Play-Along Series

Play your favorite songs quickly and easily!

Just follow the notation, listen to the CD to hear how the harmonica should sound, and then play along using the separate full-band backing tracks. The melody and lyrics are also included in the book in case you want to sing, or to simply help you follow along. The audio CD is playable on any CD player. For PC and Mac computer users, the CD is enhanced so you can adjust the recording to any tempo without changing pitch!

HAL•LEONARD®
CORPORATION
7777 W. BLUEMOUND RD. P.O. BOX 13819
MILWAUKEE, WISCONSIN 53213

www.halleonard.com

1. Pop/Rock
And When I Die • Bright Side of the Road • I Should Have Known Better • Low Rider • Miss You • Piano Man • Take the Long Way Home • You Don't Know How It Feels.
00000478....................................$14.99

2. Rock Hits
Cowboy • Hand in My Pocket • Karma Chameleon • Middle of the Road • Run Around • Smokin' in the Boys Room • Train in Vain • What I like About You.
00000479....................................$14.99

3. Blues/Rock
Big Ten Inch Record • On the Road Again • Roadhouse Blues • Rollin' and Tumblin' • Train Kept A-Rollin' • Train, Train • Waitin' for the Bus • You Shook Me.
00000481 ....$14.99

4. Folk/Rock
Blowin' in the Wind • Catch the Wind • Daydream • Eve of Destruction • Me and Bobby McGee • Mr. Tambourine Man • Pastures of Plenty.
00000482....................................$14.99

5. Country Classics
Blue Bayou • Don't Tell Me Your Troubles • He Stopped Loving Her Today • Honky Tonk Blues • If You've Got the Money (I've Got the Time) • The Only Daddy That Will Walk the Line • Orange Blossom Special • Whiskey River.
00001004....................................$14.99

6. Country Hits
Ain't Goin' down ('Til the Sun Comes Up) • Drive (For Daddy Gene) • Getcha Some • Here's a Quarter (Call Someone Who Cares) • Honkytonk U • One More Last Chance • Put Yourself in My Shoes • Turn It Loose.
00001013....................................$14.99

9. Chicago Blues
Blues with a Feeling • Easy • Got My Mo Jo Working • Help Me • I Ain't Got You • Juke • Messin' with the Kid.
00001091....................................$14.99

10. Blues Classics
Baby, Scratch My Back • Eyesight to the Blind • Good Morning Little Schoolgirl • Honest I Do • I'm Your Hoochie Coochie Man • My Babe • Ride and Roll • Sweet Home Chicago.
00001093....................................$14.99

11. Christmas Carols
Angels We Have Heard on High • Away in a Manger • Deck the Hall • The First Noel • Go, Tell It on the Mountain • Jingle Bells • Joy to the World • O Little Town of Bethlehem.
00001296....................................$12.99

12. Bob Dylan
All Along the Watchtower • Blowin' in the Wind • It Ain't Me Babe • Just like a Woman • Mr. Tambourine Man • Shelter from the Storm • Tangled up in Blue • The Times They Are A-Changin'.
00001326 ....$16.99

13. Little Walter
Can't Hold Out Much Longer • Crazy Legs • I Got to Go • Last Night • Mean Old World • Rocker • Sad Hours • You're So Fine.
00001334 ....$14.99

15. Jazz Classics
All Blues • Au Privave • Comin' Home Baby • Song for My Father • Sugar • Sunny • Take Five • Work Song.
00001336 ....$14.99

16. Christmas Favorites
Blue Christmas • Frosty the Snow Man • Here Comes Santa Claus (Right down Santa Claus Lane) • Jingle-Bell Rock • Nuttin' for Christmas • Rudolph the Red-Nosed Reindeer • Santa Claus Is Comin' to Town • Silver Bells.
00001350....................................$14.99

Prices, content, and availability subject to change without notice.

0513

THE HAL LEONARD HARMONICA METHOD AND SONGBOOKS

THE METHOD

THE HAL LEONARD COMPLETE HARMONICA METHOD — CHROMATIC HARMONICA
by Bobby Joe Holman

The only harmonica method to present the chromatic harmonica in 14 scales and modes in all 12 keys! This book/CD pack will take beginners from the basics on through to the most advanced techniques available for the contemporary harmonica player. Each section contains appropriate songs and exercises (which are demonstrated on the CD) that enable the player to quickly learn the various concepts presented. Every aspect of this versatile musical instrument is explored and explained in easy-to-understand detail with illustrations. The musical styles covered include traditional, blues, pop and rock.

00841286 Book/CD Pack $12.95

THE HAL LEONARD COMPLETE HARMONICA METHOD — DIATONIC HARMONICA
by Bobby Joe Holman

The only harmonica method specific to the diatonic harmonica, covering all six positions. This book/CD pack contains over 20 songs and musical examples that take beginners from the basics on through to the most advanced techniques available for the contemporary harmonica player. Each section contains appropriate songs and exercises (which are demonstrated on the CD) that enable the player to quickly learn the various concepts presented. Every aspect of this versatile musical instrument is explored and explained in easy-to-understand detail with illustrations. The musical styles covered include traditional, blues, pop and rock.

00841285 Book/CD Pack $12.95

THE SONGBOOKS

The Hal Leonard Harmonica Songbook series offers a wide variety of music especially tailored to the two-volume Hal Leonard Harmonica Method, but can be played by all harmonica players, diatonic and chromatic alike. All books include study and performance notes, and a guide to harmonica tablature. From classical themes to Christmas music, rock and roll to Broadway, there's something for everyone!

BROADWAY SONGS FOR HARMONICA **INCLUDES TAB**
arranged by Bobby Joe Holman

19 show-stopping Broadway tunes for the harmonica. Songs include: Ain't Misbehavin' • Bali Ha'i • Camelot • Climb Ev'ry Mountain • Do-Re-Mi • Edelweiss • Give My Regards to Broadway • Hello, Dolly! • I've Grown Accustomed to Her Face • The Impossible Dream (The Quest) • Memory • Oklahoma • People • and more.

00820009 .... $9.95

CLASSICAL FAVORITES FOR HARMONICA **INCLUDES TAB**
arranged by Bobby Joe Holman

18 famous classical melodies and themes, arranged for diatonic and chromatic players. Includes: By the Beautiful Blue Danube • Clair De Lune • The Flight of the Bumble Bee • Gypsy Rondo • Moonlight Sonata • Surprise Symphony • The Swan (Le Cygne) • Waltz of the Flowers • and more, plus a guide to harmonica tablature.

00820006 .... $9.95

MOVIE FAVORITES FOR HARMONICA **INCLUDES TAB**
arranged by Bobby Joe Holman

19 songs from the silver screen, arranged for diatonic and chromatic harmonica. Includes: Alfie • Bless the Beasts and Children • Chim Chim Cher-ee • The Entertainer • Georgy Girl • Midnight Cowboy • Moon River • Picnic • Speak Softly, Love • Stormy Weather • Tenderly • Unchained Melody • What a Wonderful World • and more, plus a guide to harmonica tablature.

00820014 .... $9.95

POP **INCLUDES TAB**
arra

17 c_____monica
(eith_____raham,
Mart_____ream
Blue_____Sixteen
Cand_____y Me •
Tears_____ty Yak •
and

0082_____.. $9.95